Schwa in 1st G

by Rachel Sorsel

ISBN: 9798354051076

teacherrachel1997@gmail.com

To my 1st Grade Readers

On the first day of 1st Grade, Schwa was really shy and nervous! All of the other Letters and Sounds already knew each other from Kindergarten, but Schwa was a brand new student.

Letter A walked up to Schwa while they were putting away their lunch boxes.

"Hi, I'm A. I spell LOTS of different vowel sounds, so I'm friends with everyone in class!"

I'm Schwa!

Schwa was excited and nervous to be meeting someone who might be a friend. Maybe they could work together to spell words with Letter A??

Letter E overheard friends talking by the cubbies. He was close with Letter A, of course. They both spelled vowels.

"What kind of a letter name is schwa?" E asked.

"Oh, I'm not a letter," said Schwa. "I'm just a sound!"
Letter A and Letter E looked at each other. Schwa
could not tell what they were thinking.

"SH walked over too. "You must be like us! We are two letters that can spell a sound together!"

""I don't think so," said Schwa. "You can hear me in many words, but I'm not a letter!"

"You might spell more than one sound?" said Letter U as they all walked to sit at their desks.

"You're right! I AM more than one sound!" Schwa said excitedly, feeling like the other students were starting to understand. "I am **/ih/** and **/uh/**."

ih

uh

"That's so cool!" said Letter I. "I can also spell /i/ when I am short! You can find me in words like "big" or "sit."

"But I've never seen YOU in a word before!" said Letter A to Schwa. The rest of the class nodded in agreement. "We've read lots of books. We spell lots of words, but none of them have shapes like you!" Letter A exclaimed.

Maybe Letter A might not be a friend after all...

"The Teacher, Ms. Alphabet, cleared her throat as she listened to the conversations.
The students looked up, confused about their new classmate.

"Did you all know that you might not see the schwa symbol in words, but the schwa sounds are EVERYWHERE!" Ms. Alphabet started to explain. The consonants in the class looked especially surprised,

"Okay," said Letter A. "Then how do you even spell Schwa?"

Everyone in the class looked expectantly from Schwa to Ms. Alphabet, and then back to Schwa.

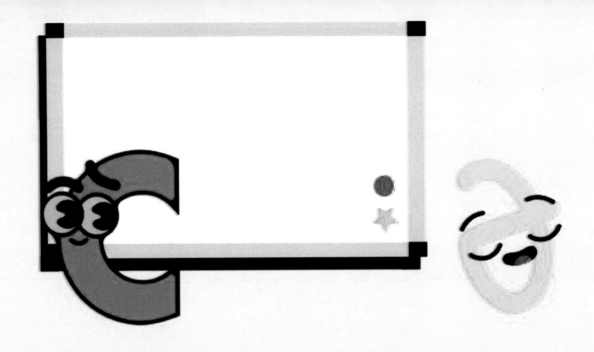

"Well," Schwa said, "I can actually be spelled in many different ways I think." C nodded quietly. She knew that /k/ and /s/ could be spelled many ways. She looked over at Letters K and S and winked.

"Precisely," said Ms. Alphabet. "Schwa can be spelled by ANY vowel."
The vowel letters looked at each other. Letter A started to blush.

salAd (ih)

bAlloon (uh)

"Yes! Letter A spells me in salAd and bAlloon," said Schwa gaining their strong speaker voice.

17

"Schwa is spelled e in carpEt and in itEm." Ms. Alphabet added.

"Oooh oooh! When do I spell Schwa?" said Letter I.
"Well, your short sound is already Schwa, /ih/! But you can spell /uh/ in pencIl!" said Ms. Alphabet.
Letter I gave Schwa a high five!

focUs (ih)   carrOt (ih)
Short u = /uh/   dinOsaur (uh)

"I am spelled o in carrOt and in dinOsaur, and even though it often spells /uh/, Letter U spells /ih/ in focUs." Schwa said bravely.

Letter U answered, "You're right. I sometimes spell /ih/!" I was so confused about that before! Now I know I was spelling schwa!"

20

"Multi-Syllabic"

Ms. Alphabet nodded. "Schwa may not be common in one syllable words, but in words with more than one syllable, all of you vowels spell Schwa so often!" "I happen on the syllable that is less loud and strong. For example, we don't say hapPEN. We say HAPpen, and that e spells me!" Schwa exclaimed. 21

"In Kindergarten, we didn't spell many longer words with many syllables yet. That's why you all didn't know about Schwa, but I'm so excited for them to be a new friend in 1st Grade! I'm sure we will work together well with them!" Ms. Alphabet smiled. Vowels AND Consonants all over the classroom smiled right at Schwa.

"I may be a brand new student," thought Schwa,
"But, wow I feel so important already!"

About the Author

Rachel is a 1st Grade Teacher just like Ms. Alphabet. She loves to teach reading and also teaches theatre. She loves singing, the color yellow, and her cat, Rochambeau!

Learn more about phonics in "And Sometimes Y"

Coming Soon: Short Vowel Protectors

78499792R00019